Andante and Caprice

CLARINET QUARTET

1st Bb Clarinet

C. W. von GLUCK
Arr. by Clair W. Johnson

Andante and Caprice
CLARINET QUARTET

2nd Bb Clarinet

C. W. von GLUCK
Arr. by Clair W. Johnson

Andante and Caprice
CLARINET QUARTET

3rd Bb Clarinet

C. W. von GLUCK
Arr. by Clair W. Johnson

2057-4

Andante and Caprice

CLARINET QUARTET

4th Bb Clarinet
(Bass Clarinet)

C. W. von GLUCK
Arr. by Clair W. Johnson

2057-4